Rainbow Warrior ARTISTS

NATIVE ARTISTS of EUROPE

Reavis Moore

John Muir Publications
Santa Fe, New Mexico

Dedicated to my Mom, Kay Moore, for believing.

Deepest thanks to Eliza Gilkyson, Cordelia Gilkyson and all my family for their love and support during my long journies away from home, and to my step-son Cisco Gilliland for his invaluable assistance in researching this book and helping me keep it together on the road. Also thanks to all the people in Europe who pointed me in the right direction, took me in, fed me, tried to talk English with me, and made me laugh; and to all my ancestors from Ireland, Scotland, England, and France who kept our creative traditions alive.

Special thanks to the artists, Eilín, Xabier, Lis, Lídia, Lars, and their families for sharing their lives with me.

John Muir Publications, P.O. Box 613, Santa Fe, New Mexico 87504

CURR
N
6750
.M66
1994

Typefaces: Benguiat, Kabel
Illustrations: Chris Brigman
Design: Ken Wilson
Typography: Marcie Pottern
Printer: Guynes Printing Company
Bindery: Prizma Industries, Inc.

Distributed to the book trade by
W. W. Norton & Co., Inc.
500 Fifth Avenue
New York, New York 10110

Distributed to the education market by
The Wright Group
19201 120th Avenue N.E.
Bothell, Washington 98011

CONTENTS

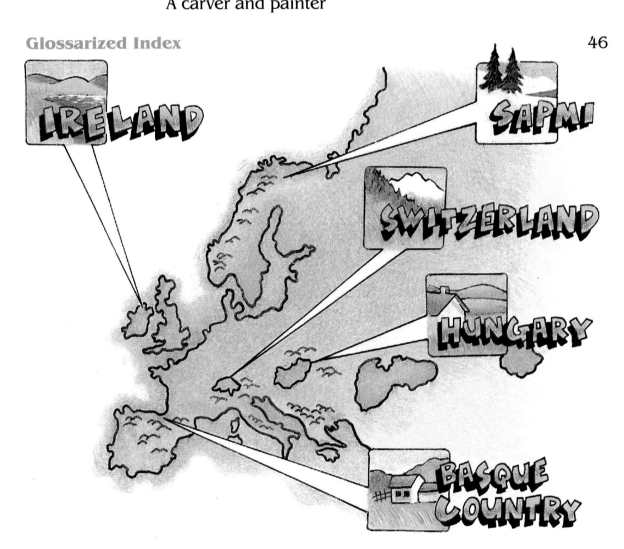

FOREWORD BY LEVAR BURTON

What is creativity? I'm sure it means something different to almost everyone, so I'll give you my definition. Creativity is that brilliant spark of life inside of me that I express in the world. How I express that creative spark is what defines me as an artist, whether it's acting or writing or telling someone how I feel in a conversation. These are all true forms of creative expression.

You might feel creative when you're painting, singing, playing basketball, or cooking. My point is this: there is no one way to be creative. Creativity has as many faces as there are human beings on the planet. It is the job of the artist to discover what form of expression suits her or him best and then create from a place of joy. That is the key. We know we are on the creative path when what we do brings us joy.

Have you ever noticed how your own moods tend to affect those around you? How your good mood can help cheer up your best friend when he or she is feeling sad? The same is true when we express ourselves creatively. As artists, when we create from that pure place of joy, we have the ability to inspire those around us to discover their own creative spark. This is the miracle of creativity. This is how we change the world.

In the Rainbow Warrior Artists series you will meet remarkable individuals from around the world. You will hear them talk about creativity and how they express it in their lives. It is my hope that their stories will help fan your creative spark into a brilliant flame that helps to light the way for all of us.

INTRODUCTION

This is the third book in the Rainbow Warrior Artists series. This series profiles native artists from around the world. In the first book we crisscross North America, visiting five traditional Native American artists. In the second book we journey through Africa, from Morocco in the north to Lesotho in the south, meeting five native African artists.

In this book we circle the edges of Europe to find the last of an almost lost traditional artistic culture. We start in southwest Ireland, then pass through the Basque country of Spain and France. From there we cross the Alps into Switzerland before heading east to Hungary. Our last stop is in far northern Sweden in the land of Sapmi, home of the Saamis, Europe's last true tribal people.

On this journey we look into the culture and history of the people of these lands. We then spend time with the artists in their home countries, learning their life stories and sharing their creative understanding. Along the way we meet a singer-drummer-storyteller, a painter-poet, a musician-singer-songwriter, a ceramicist-painter, and a carver-painter. All of the artists share a deep love for their work and a heartfelt connection to the traditions of their people.

It is impossible to communicate the beauty of these artists, their cultures, and their lands with the few words and photographs in this book. But perhaps these glimpses of European art and life will inspire you to learn more about your own traditional culture.

A CREATIVE LIFE

All of us humans are creative beings. Creativity is not just painting, dancing, playing music, or one of the other well-known arts. Creativity can also be found in everyday activities, such as talking or cooking. How we fix up our room is a form of creative expression. Even in the way we walk we can be creative. (Watch how different people walk and you'll see what I mean!).

Living a creative life means first waking up to the fact that you are a creative person. Become aware of all that you create, positive and negative, in your life. Knowing what you already create will help you increase the creativity in your life.

Be patient with yourself as you explore your creative nature. It takes time and effort to create something of beauty. Creativity is not a competition with other people to see who is better. It is a competition with yourself to see if you can improve on what you have already created.

Ultimately, your artwork is how you live, what you do, and how you relate to others. If you work hard you can create the life you want. You will have setbacks along the way, as we all do. But if you keep trying, if you keep smiling, you will find the strength to carry on. One day you will be able to look back on your life and see how much you have created. Then it will be your turn to share what you've learned with the next generation of children.

This is my creation for you, a book full of beautiful people in beautiful places making beautiful things. I hope it helps you to see the beauty of your own life and inspires you to become fully the creative being that you truly are. Dreams do come true. It can happen to you.

IRISH LAND AND PEOPLE

On the western edge of Europe, across the Atlantic Ocean from America, is the magical island of Ireland. Green is the color of Ireland. Springs, streams, and rivers, fed by year-round rains, help grow the lush green grasses that cover the rolling hills and valleys. With the wisdom of countless generations, the people understand that the land belongs to them and they belong to the land.

The first people here, hunters and gatherers of food, were nomads who moved with the seasons to survive. As the centuries passed, the people became more settled and turned to farming and raising animals. Eventually, most of the trees were cut down to make space for growing crops and grazing sheep. Today, despite the growth of modern cities such as Dublin and Belfast, Ireland is still an agricultural nation. And for most of the people, the old tradition of caring for the land that feeds them and nurtures their spirits continues.

A stream on the Dingle Peninsula

"When I was young I didn't have any interest in the old-style singing. Now traditional music is my favorite kind."

—Eilín Ní Chearna

The culture and folklore of Ireland is as alive and rich as its soil. This is the land of mythical leprechauns and screaming banshees. Poets, musicians, and storytellers are the heart of Irish culture. Every great and small moment in Irish history is remembered in poems, songs, and stories. Love, marriage, birth, and death are the subjects of countless tales told. Before there were books there were bards. Their job was to pass on the old stories, the history of the people, and to make new stories for future generations.

The migrations of the Irish people are legendary. Millions of people of Irish descent live in America today. Many of these families came during a famine in the 1800s when the Irish potato crop failed. For poor farmers, starving or leaving was the only choice. More recently, young Irish women and men have fanned out throughout Europe to find work.

An Irish stonemason

The political history of Ireland is filled with sorrow. Many people have died fighting for Ireland's independence. Even though it is an island, protected by the sea, it has been invaded many times. One of the earliest invasions of Ireland was carried out by the Celtic tribes that once controlled most of central Europe. Although they ruled Ireland for many centuries, it is said that over time the Celts became Irish themselves, and that much of the Irish culture was preserved as a result.

In the 1100s, England invaded Ireland. It controlled the entire country until the people of southern Ireland rose up in 1916. Unlike the Celts, the British brought many unwanted changes to Irish society. One of these was forcing the people to speak English instead of Gaelic, the ancient Irish language. Children were often harshly punished for speaking their native tongue. Despite British efforts to do away with it, the Irish language survived and is again being taught in the schools. However, the British still control northern Ireland, where a bloody civil war continues to this day.

An ancient standing stone with Celtic symbols

Eilín working at Raidio na Gaeltachta

EILÍN NÍ CHEARNA

Eilín Ní Chearna (EYE-leen nee KEE-ar-nah) was born in 1956 in the small village of Muirioch (MAH-reek, which means "the sea"). It is on the Dingle Peninsula in southwest Ireland.

I had a nice childhood. There was no television, no electricity, and no telephone. I didn't even know things like that existed. We used oil lamps for light. There were no toys until I was nine or ten and Santa Claus started coming. I just played outside with other kids. We made mud cakes and played in the ruins of an old house.

Eilín's parents came from the Blasket Islands a few miles off the tip of the Dingle Peninsula. Long after most of Ireland had become modernized, people on the islands were still living a very traditional way of life.

The islands were isolated from the rest of the world. Of course there were no telephones. They didn't even have radios or any way to communicate with the mainland. They were fishermen who used small boats made of canvas that looked like canoes. My father would go out all night in his little boat with just a compass. They also had sheep and a few cows. Their main source of food was fish, wild game such as rabbits, and vegetables from their gardens, mainly potatoes, cabbage, and carrots. They lived in stone houses. It was very primitive.

The people worked hard, but they loved their lives. They carried on the old ways as if the rest of the world didn't exist.

They were very happy there. They would have ball nights in the house. People would come over, they would make music, sing, dance, and tell stories.

Over the years people moved away from the islands. In the mid-1950s the government moved the last of the people onto Dingle Peninsula,

Eilín and her family

because there were no medical services on the islands. The islands became nature preserves, and many of the traditional ways continued on the mainland.

The traditional life was all Eilin knew as a child.

I didn't learn English till I was about 11. No one spoke English until the tourists came in the summers. The kids all know English now.

Eventually, Eilín got married. She and her husband John, who is a potter, have two little girls, Sinead (SHIN-ade) and Darina (dah-REEN-ah). They live close to where Eilin grew up.

From their backyard the land slopes gently to the ocean, and the Blasket Islands can be seen in the distance. Although she hasn't gone far from the islands where her ancestors lived, the world they knew is almost gone.

Eilín's mother

Today everything is so homogenized by television. Nobody talks to anybody anymore. People don't visit each other in their houses, or do storytelling at the fire. As the old saying goes, "There's

no hearth like your own hearth." That's all gone. I would have hated to miss that. We used to get together a lot.

Boats in Dingle Harbor

Eilín playing the bohron

SINGING THE OLD STORIES ANEW

Eilin is a traditional Irish singer and drummer. Her work is helping to preserve the old stories and songs of her people. She also works at Raidio na Gaeltachta (RAH-dee-oh nah GEHL-tuhk-tah), an Irish language radio station.

Her father was a singer in the pubs, and her mother would sing around the house. Though she grew up with traditional music all around her, like many children she was interested in what was new.

When I was young I used to stand in front of my mirror and pretend that I was singing. But I didn't have any interest in the sean nos (SHAHN nohs), which is the old-style singing. When I was 15 I went to work in a public house (pub). They encouraged me to sing. Back then I only knew one old song. They had a bohron (BAH-rohn, a traditional Irish drum) and I began to play it. Now traditional music is my favorite kind.

In the old days playing music and singing were not professions. They were part of people's daily lives. They sang and told stories to teach, to entertain, and to mark special occasions. Eilín sings for the same reasons today. But times have changed.

When I started I was very shy. I didn't have much confidence. I still can't say I like to sing in public. But last year I won the Oireachtas (oh-ROCK-tis) all-Irish singing competition, and I've been giving concerts around Ireland and Scotland. Now people expect a lot more from me, and I get asked to sing everywhere I go. I don't like the pressure of competitions and concerts. In the old days people sang around the house, at weddings, or in the pub. People weren't forward, they didn't like pushing themselves out front.

The sign of Raidio na Gaeltachta

The Atlantic Ocean and coastline of Dingle Peninsula

Eilín's singing and playing come naturally, from deep inside her.

I don't think about singing. I just feel it and sing to myself. I close my eyes when I sing. When there's a concert coming up I get kind of anxious. But once I've sung the song I feel great. I think, "I've done it, what was I so nervous about?"

To Eilín choosing the right song is as important as singing well.

Sometimes I hear a song and I like the air of it, the melody. Then I must get the words to it and learn it. But I'm very lazy about learning songs! I have to really feel it to want to learn it.

Eilín's songs are pathways back through time. She tells the tales that are the history of her people. She sings the words and music passed down from generation to generation, connecting the past with the present.

I learned the words to one song from my father shortly before he died. Sometimes when I'm singing it I think of him and where he is and what he's doing. I remember sitting on his bed that day, learning the words, and I wonder how he would feel about my getting on so good with my singing.

KEEP DOING IT

Each of you has talents that are uniquely your own. Sometimes your talents and interests are similar to your parents'. Other times you may have your own special gifts shared by no one else in your family. Finding out what you can do and what you really want to do are the first steps on the creative path.

For Eilín it was learning the old stories and music that sparked her desire to be a singer and a drummer. Like her father, she knew she had to sing. For you it may be dancing, drawing, or another artistic form that interests you. No one but you can decide what to do with your life. Other people can help and encourage you, but it's really up to you to find the courage to do what you want to do.

Listen closely to Eilín's message. Her words will help you with whatever creative adventures you choose.

Enjoy yourself with music or whatever else interests you. If you're too shy to do it front of people, keep at it. I was in my thirties before I felt comfortable singing in public. If people are telling you you're good at something, keep doing it. If you keep doing it, as you get older you won't be that shy. It may be a burden for a while. It will be hard at times. But continue on and after a while it won't be that hard. Eventually, you will enjoy it more and more.

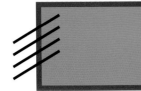

STORIES INTO SONGS

The songs Eilín sings are stories. Someone put each of these stories to music. This activity is a chance for you to tell a story in a song and be a songwriter.

You will need the following things:
- A pencil with an eraser.
- Several sheets of lined paper.
- A tape player.

Step 1. Ask an adult you know (a family member or a friend) to tell you a short, simple story from the past. It can be a childhood story, or a story about your town or any other kind of interesting story. It helps if the story is funny or sad.

Step 2. Have the storyteller tell you the story several times. After you know it well, write the important parts down using as few words as possible.

Step 3. Now go off by yourself and work on telling the story with fewer and fewer words. Use strong words that bring pictures to mind. Rewrite the story as many times as you need to. Go back to the storyteller and check for mistakes.

Step 4. Now put the words to music. Choose a song you like. Listen to a tape of it several times. If the song has words, try not to listen to them. Focus on the melody, the music. Now turn off the music and hum the melody. When you know the melody by heart, go to the next step.

Step 5. Try singing the words of the story to the melody you've chosen. You will probably have to take some words out so the story fits the melody. Don't worry about making the words rhyme, just sing the words to the story. When you know it well (don't worry about memorizing, read what you've written), go back to the storyteller and sing the story for her or him. Ask the storyteller if any changes are needed. Sing it to your friends. Now try writing a song about one of your own stories. Try making up the music yourself.

XABIER SOUBELET
of Basque Country

BASQUE LAND AND PEOPLE

In northwest Spain and southwest France, stretching from the beaches of the Atlantic Coast into the Pyrenees Mountains is the region known as Basque (bask) country.

Ancient towns made of hand-cut stone sit atop hills that slope gently into valleys. Clear streams and raging rivers run through green pastures, passing perfectly tended vineyards.

Flocks of white wooly sheep, watched by quiet men in black berets with wooden staffs, meander through a land that seems to belong to an earlier time. The pace here is slow, and the countryside is silent except for the sounds of nature.

But in these very fields fierce battles have raged. The history of the Basque people, during their 7,000 years here, is stained with the terror of invaders from other lands. Empire-building armies of Visigoths, Arabs, Castillians (Spanish), and French have all passed through this land.

The Basque village of Arraioz

"*Because of my painting I have developed a special relationship with nature. It's a circle. Painting helps me understand nature and nature helps me understand painting.*"

—Xabier Soubelet

14

The outsiders wanted to possess the natural riches and beauty of this place. Some captured the land for a while, laying waste to the countryside and the people. Others barely penetrated its boundaries. None were able to completely defeat the ferocious Basque fighters, who carried the power of their ancestors who had lived and died on this soil. Territory was lost and won, but the spirit of the people was never conquered.

Mercedes and Pilar, two Basque women

Today the Basque country is still not free. In fact, it is not even a nation. Its lands are part of the nations of Spain and France. The struggle for independence continues. Basque fighters wage a campaign to secede from Spain, while Basque political leaders work peacefully for the same goal. Despite the difficulty and uncertainty of their cause, the Basque people believe that they will one day achieve their freedom.

The Basque way of life is rooted in the land, like the trees and the grape vines. These are people who do not move to the rapid rhythm of European civilization. They live in tune with the slow and steady beat of nature and the seasons. They walk and talk with the confidence of those who are part of the land they live on. Family and friendship are as lasting as the land.

The telling of stories old and new, with the help of a little Basque red wine, is an age-old pastime that often brings laughter and tears. When a stranger walks among the Basque he doesn't walk alone for long. The respect they give to each other is also extended to the traveler who enters their world with an open heart and mind.

The Basques' love of art is as old as the cave paintings in the hills where their ancestors once lived. Basque art and handicraft are famous throughout

Basque ponies

the world. From wood carvings to abstract oil paintings, the artists of Basque country are innovators as well as carriers of tradition. Their art is tied to the power of nature.

Looking at a Basque landscape painting splashed with greens, yellows, blues, and reds, you see the fluid forms of trees, rivers, mountains, and sky. This is the beauty of nature lovingly and gently captured by the hand of one who understands her.

15

Xabier and his daughters

XABIER SOUBELET

Xabier Soubelet (zah-BEE-air sue-BAH-let) was born in 1953, in the town of Saint Jean de Luz in French Basque country, near the border with Spain. Xabier's father is French Basque and his mother is Spanish Basque. He is their only child. Xabier's mother died when he was five years old. As a child he spent much time at his mother's family home in Arraioz (ah-ROY-ohs), in Spain.

My mother's family home is over 300 years old. Our family has been there for over 200 years. Arraioz is a small town of only 200 people. As a child I used to play in the river there and in the mountains where we went to look for mushrooms. In Saint Jean de Luz I played at the beach and played sports like football (soccer).

As a child Xabier spoke French and Spanish as well as his native Basque language. When he was 14 he went to England to learn English. He went to an all-boys school in France until he was 16, where his love of language and literature grew.

I went to a boarding school during the week. I didn't like math or science. I liked language and writing. We all read The Fantastic Adventures of Jules Verne. *I was a jubilant boy. My friends and I were very funny. I didn't like the fact that there were no girls at the school. But in this period the friendships were very strong. I still see some of those friends today.*

Xabier also had a strong love of music. He listened to the Beatles (John was his favorite). He began to play music when he was 15. He played the guitar, trumpet, piano, and *txistu* (CHEES-too), which is a Basque wind instrument.

Xabier's family home

I liked to play everything, but in my youth I didn't like to study the mathematics of music. I wrote poetry and songs about life and death.

Xabier went on to university to further study the Spanish and Basque languages. But between high school and university, when he was 17, he had to spend a year in the French military, doing his national service.

Xabier painting in his yard

It was very bad, but at least I got to play trumpet in a military band.

He met his future wife, Katte (CAT-tee), when he was 22.

We met at a fiesta. As soon as I met her, I knew she was the one. We were married two years later.

They now have two girls, nine-year-old Maitena (MY-tay-nah) and five-year-old Iduzki (EE-doo-skee).

Since 1981 Xabier has been teaching Basque and Spanish language, and art, at a high school in Saint Jean de Luz.

I like teaching. It's important to be with young people to see that being young is the same today. The world reality is different. Their problems are different, but basically we're the same. But I don't spend all my time teaching. During my off time I paint. I think that in ten years I will leave the school to paint and write full-time.

Xabier and his mentor, Jose Mari Apazatxei (right)

Basque countryside

A NATURAL VISION OF ART

Xabier is a painter. His medium is oil paints. He is continuing an old and respected tradition of Basque nature painters. He also comes from a family of artists.

There are many artists on both sides of my family. My mother's sister and two of my father's brothers are painters, and many cousins are painters.

When Xabier was young he was interested in other types of creative expression and didn't try painting. But in his early adulthood he discovered a passion for painting that has stayed with him throughout his life.

I didn't start painting until I was 22. I always had a strong feeling or sensibility inside me for art. This is very important. I expressed it with poetry and music. But because I met many painters, I became interested and began to paint.

He never studied painting. Instead he spent time with other painters, watching them work and talking with them. This is part of the old tradition of learning directly from others.

One of the painters I met, Jose Mari Apazatxei (ah-PEZ-ah-chi-ah), helped me with my painting, like a friend. We painted together and he gave me advice about my work. He has been a very good teacher and friend for me. We still paint together often.

Nature is Xabier's source of inspiration. He paints in the mountains and along the streams in the valleys near his home.

Xabier painting

As a painter you must like nature. Because in nature there are all the colors and all the forms. In every style of painting there is color and form. Using these a painter can then interpret things as he chooses. Because of my painting I have developed a special relationship with nature. It's a circle. Painting helps me understand nature and nature helps me under-stand painting.

One of Xabier's paintings

As an artist, Xabier has a way of seeing and then capturing what he sees in a painting. This gift of vision and creation are at the heart of all artistic expression.

My paintings are first made in my mind, before they are realized on canvas. It is a special vision that I have. First something in nature catches my eye. At that time I begin to see the painting form within my mind. Then as I paint I see the vision created before me.

For some people two and two is four, for a mathematician or scientist, for instance. This is sensible for them. For me, two and two is not four! Two ideas and two ideas do not make four ideas. These ideas together make something greater. That's just the way I see things. It isn't a better way, it's just different.

For Xabier painting is a doorway. Through this door is a land where time stands still in a place where the beauty of nature is revealed.

When I am painting I don't see the time pass. I enter another world, a world of this moment. This is part of the force of creativity that is living in the world. It is a peaceful force that stands for nature and beauty.

SAVE THE WORLD

Xabier's life has been dedicated to unfolding that creative part of himself. From the time he was a young boy he knew he had something to express. In your life you too have something to express. Finding yourself and your expression will take time and patience. For Xabier it took until he was 22 to discover his gift as a painter.

By studying the ideas and works of others, the way Xabier studied other painters, you may be able to find inspiration for yourself.

You must go your own way. But first you must choose the way that you are going to go. It is important that you love what you do and love what you make.

If you choose to live a creative life, you will find difficulties as well as many rewards. One of the difficulties that many artists face is how to create beauty in a world where there is so much injustice and hatred. Xabier has also faced this question. For him the answers have come from nature and from his own heart. Perhaps you will find in his words something to help you with your own quest to understand.

We must make a better world, a world where we relate to nature, and more naturally relate to each other. Within you, in your own human nature, is creativity and love. This creativity and love, expressed in everything you do, can help save the world.

FREE FORM DRAWING

No matter how talented you are at drawing, Xabier believes this actitivity can help you draw even better.

You will need the following things:
- A pencil with an eraser.
- A few sheets of blank paper.

Step 1. Find a quiet place where you can be alone, maybe in nature. Take out a piece of paper and a pencil. Imagine shapes you could draw on the paper. Squares, circles, triangles, and rectangles are a few different kinds of shapes. You can mix these shapes, like joining together part of a square and part of a circle. You can use wavy lines and straight lines. Draw whatever shapes you imagine. Draw freely. Don't worry about what it looks like, or how big or small it is. Draw as many shapes on as many pieces of paper as you want.

Step 2. Choose one of the shapes that you especially like. Spend some time studying it. What does it look like to you? Does it look like something in nature or maybe something in your house? Does it remind you of an animal or a person? Next think about what lines you could add to the shape to make it look more like what it reminds you of. Add the lines that will make it become something anyone could recognize. Take chances. If you make a mistake, erase it and try again. Keep working on it until it really looks like something.

Step 3. When you have finished turning your shape into something, show it to your family or friends. Try doing it again. You may find that each time you do this activity it gets easier and the pictures you draw get better.

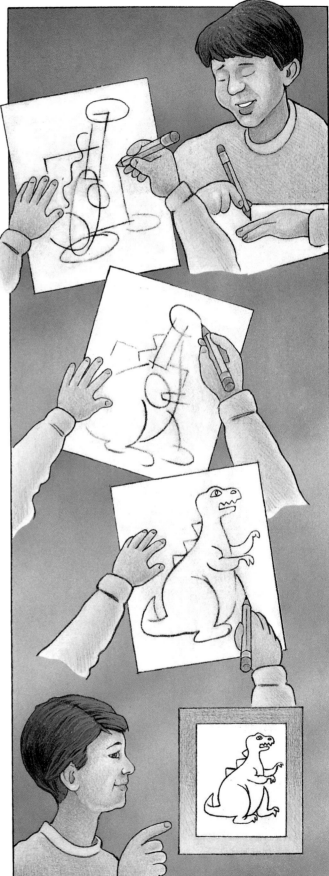

LIS GLARIS
of Switzerland

SWISS LAND AND PEOPLE

East of France, south of Germany, north of Italy, and west of Austria lies the hidden highlands called Switzerland. Towering snow-capped mountain peaks gaze down upon languid crystal blue lakes. Here human life moves with the precision and simplicity of seconds ticking away on an old reliable clock.

Although it is surrounded by large and powerful nations, Switzerland has built a unique national independence. Within the natural defenses of the Alps Mountains, Switzerland remained neutral while two world wars raged all around its borders.

There is very little poverty in Switzerland. The people of this tiny country have created one of the strongest economies in the world. Swiss watches, chocolates, cheeses, and throat lozenges are just a few of the things that Switzerland is famous for around the world.

In addition to business, the Swiss have helped lead the world in art, music, psychology, and ecology. While they have pursued

The town of Glarus

*"**F**ind out about yourself, apart from what is modern. Find what you want. Don't copy. Find your traditions and express them in your own unique way."*

—Lis Glaris

wealth, they have also kept in tune with the Earth. As a result, Switzerland possesses a beautiful and pristine natural environment where water and land is as important as time and money.

Swiss history is the story of diverse cultures coming together to form a nation. Over 5,000 years ago farming settlements were established in Switzerland. Two thousand years ago a Celtic tribe called the Helvetians settled here. Also around this time the area became part of the Roman Empire. Various Germanic tribes also migrated to Switzerland, as did tribes from southeastern France.

The Alps above Glarus

Beginning 700 years ago these various groups, living in different parts of the country, came together to form a confederacy that became Switzerland. Today four languages are spoken here, German, French, Italian, and Romansch.

Most of the Swiss people now live in and around modern cities such as Zurich, Geneva, Bern, Lucerne, and Basel. But if you travel just a little ways into the mountains you will find small towns, villages, and clusters of farms that are far from modern.

In fact, in the mountains life goes on much as it has for hundreds of years. Cows and goats wander the countryside. Traditional dress is worn on special occasions and traditional musical instruments, such as the Alpine horns, are still in use. The old folk songs and stories still serve to educate children about life. And the mountains still receive and echo back the lonesome sound of the solitary yodeler.

No one knows how long the traditional Swiss lifestyle will survive. In this century, many young people from these mountain areas have moved to the city and chosen other careers besides farming. Some feel that modern farming methods and competition from other countries will mean the end of the traditional Swiss farmer. But the strength, determination, and individuality of the mountain families, whose ancestors cleared and settled these rocky lands, seems an equal match for the challenges of the twenty-first century.

An old Swiss steam locomotive

Lis playing music with her cousin and father

LIS GLARIS

Lis Glaris (GLAH-ris) was born in the very old town of Glarus, which means "clear ice." Before the people came, the valley was filled with glacier ice. Glarus is in a valley surrounded by the Alps.

This is my valley. My family has lived in this very house for six generations. There are many stories from this place. The last witch lived here about 200 years ago. Her name

was Anna Goldie. She was not a bad person, but the church said she was a witch and she was burned. You can still hear her cries when the wind blows!

Many of the stories Lis heard as a child have been passed down through the generations to help guide the children through life.

This is a story about Mount Glarnish. There was once a young girl named Farina who wanted to go up on the mountain. The people told her, "Don't go, the snow is coming!" But she was not listening and went up to the top. While she was up there it started to snow, and she was trapped and died there. To this day that place at the top of the mountain is called the garden of Farina, and there is snow there all year round.

When Lis was a child she sang and danced for herself.

As a child I was shy. Different from now! I wanted to be a ballerina. But the women said, "Dancing is nothing. You have to go into the kitchen for

cooking and then you marry." I like to cook, but I wanted to dance.

Lis did become a dancer. When she was in her early twenties she toured Europe, dancing in her own show.

At the beginning of the show I came out dressed as an old Swiss woman in traditional clothes, dancing, singing, and yodeling in the old way. Then right there on the stage I

Lis' family home

Lis and her cousin Corinne in the mountains above Glarus

changed into a modern woman dancer and singer. I performed in Brussels, Amsterdam, Paris, Milan, all over Europe.

Her dance career was cut short when she had a car accident while on tour.

I broke both my legs. I was in the hospital and a woman said to me, "You're 28, you should get married." Shortly after that my boyfriend and I did get married.

She and her husband lived in Glarus and built a house next to her old family home. During this time Lis lived a quiet life. She raised two children, Robert and Jasmine. And as the women had predicted when Lis was a child, she did a lot of cooking.

But things were about to change. She and her husband broke up, and she again became a performer, this time with a mission to help revive interest in the old folk music of Switzerland.

My life has been a little different from many other women's, because I always did what I wanted to do.

Lis' zither

THE STRINGS OF TRADITION

Lis is a musician, a singer, and a songwriter who has committed herself to preserving the traditional music of her land.

I play the zither, which is a 15-string instrument. My father, Joachim, plays the zither also. He learned from his mother. It is one of the original instruments of Switzerland. It used to be played on a stone table, which creates a beautiful sound. The zither has been played in my valley for a long, long time. The weather is so cold here in the winter that people stay inside. As a result many people learned music. But in the last fifty years the young people didn't play as much, because they thought, "This is an old instrument, for old people, we don't like it anymore!"

Like her father, Lis is a yodeler. Yodeling is very old. Originally it was used to communicate from one mountain valley to another. One sound meant everything was all right, another told of trouble.

My father was a beautiful yodeler. When I was three or four years old we went to a big restaurant, full of people, very loud. There were no microphones then. He began to sing and yodel with the concertina and everyone became very quiet.

Like many artists, Lis found that some of her most creative work was inspired by difficulties in her life.

When my husband and I broke up, I was sad. I wrote songs to help my pain. They came out from a deep, sad heart. At this time I did not know I would ever make a recording. I just wrote for myself. Still today they are my best songs.

Then Lis decided she wanted to make a tape of the songs with the zither. But she had no money.

I went to the bank and they said, "We won't give you money for this music." This was twenty years ago and, to them, I was just a woman. So I took a mortgage on

Lis playing the zither

26

Lis plucking the strings of the zither

my house. I made the tape and sold it on the street and at fairs. And people liked it! So I made more. Now when I see that banker it makes me very happy, because he knows I am successful.

For 15 years Lis and her father had a studio where they taught children how to play the zither and other traditional instruments. They didn't take money for their work. They felt it was important for the children to learn the old music. Lis also helped other traditional musicians find work and opportunities for their music to be heard. She represented other musicians from her valley and put together shows for them.

Twenty years ago I set out to catch the young people's interest. We made recordings with new arrangements of old songs and old instruments, and it worked. We've sold many of them. I've made nine albums since then, and today there is much more interest in traditional Swiss music.

There are many goats in Switzerland

27

FIND WHAT YOU WANT

Lis has overcome many obstacles and endured many hardships in her life. No matter what happened she didn't give up. If one thing wasn't working she tried something else. Now she is successful at what she does and is loved and respected by many people. Her music is an inspiration to those who value the folk traditions of Switzerland. She is a woman who loves what she does.

Her advice to you may help you with your own problems, so that one day you can reach your dreams.

Find out about yourself, apart from what is modern. Find what you want. Don't copy. Find your traditions and express them in your own unique way. Each person must find his or her own way.

Lis feels that whatever you do you must take it seriously. If you are learning to play an instrument or learning some other type of art, remember, someone is paying for you to learn.

Fathers and mothers work hard for things for you. Respect what you are given. And parents should remember to praise their children when they do something well. I always compliment my children when they do well, and I give them a reward for their efforts. There is a reason for everything you do—a reason to go to school, a reason to brush your teeth.

Parents should explain to their children why they must do certain things. If you understand why you are doing something, you will enjoy it more and do it better.

Lis in her garden

ALMOST YODELING

Yodeling is an old form of communicating. Swiss yodelers send their voices out across the mountain valleys and hear them return as they bounce off the rocks. If you have never heard yodeling, it's hard to imagine what it sounds like. Yodelers sing very high and very low notes, quickly jumping from one to the other. Learning to yodel takes time and practice. But the idea behind yodeling is simple. You can see how it works by trying this exercise.

Step 1. Find a place where your voice echoes when you sing or speak loudly. This could be a canyon, a stairwell, a gymnasium, an empty room, or a bathroom.

Step 2. Say your name loudly and quickly. It will echo back. If you are in a big empty space, it will echo back slowly. If you are in a small space, it will echo back fast. Now sing your favorite song and listen to how the sound comes back. Your voice will sound bigger and more powerful than it normally does.

Step 3. Now sing the word "yodel" using the same musical note for each syllable, with the accent on the "YO." Now sing "YO-del-ay" all on the same note. Now sing "YO-del-ay-EE," with the accents on the "YO" and the "EE." Make the "EE" sound a higher musical note, and hold it longer. Now sing "YO-del-ay-EE-tee" and make the "tee" note a little lower than the "EE" note.

Step 4. Sing the first syllable, "YO," again. Listen to it echo. Now sing the second syllable, "del," and hear it's echo. Do the same with each syllable and listen to what they sound like.

Step 5. Now sing the syllables "YO-del-ay-EE-tee" one right after the other. Sing them slowly and listen to them echo back to you. Now sing them faster and louder. Try yodeling in different places. Try it loud and soft. To really learn how to yodel, find a tape of Swiss yodeling.

BARTH LÍDIA
of Hungary

HUNGARIAN LAND AND PEOPLE

In Eastern Europe, surrounded by Slovakia, Ukraine, Romania, the former Yugoslavia, Croatia, Slovenia, and Austria, is the old and new nation of Hungary. This is a country of overwhelming natural beauty. In the west is the vast, spring-fed Lake Balaton, which hosts thousands of rare wild birds and is near a hot mineral water lake. In the southeast is the great plain, crisscrossed by great rivers, where agriculture flourishes. In the south and the north are majestic mountain ranges with forests of oak and beech trees.

Even in the capital city of Budapest, nature holds court. The legendary Danube River lazily flows through the city, and dozens of healing, hot mineral springs bubble up into outdoor and indoor pools. Respecting nature and preserving it for future generations is a very old tradition in Hungary.

The Hungarian people were once a small tribe who came from the east to settle in their present home-land.

"I think that there are only a few people in the world who can do something they really love. I love what I do and what I make. I feel very lucky."

—Barth Lídia

A traditional Hungarian thatched-roof home

30

Hungary has been a nation for more than 1,000 years. It was long ruled by kings who fought valiantly against invaders from other lands such as Mongolia and Turkey. At the beginning of the twentieth century, it was an empire whose boundaries stretched south all the way to the Adriatic Sea and north into what is now Slovakia.

A *Hungarian man with his horse and wagon*

In World War I, Hungary was an ally of Germany. After suffering a terrible defeat, large parts of the country were taken away in a treaty written by the victorious nations, including England, France, Russia, and the United States.

When World War II broke out, Hungary was again allied with Germany in hopes of winning back its lost lands. But this didn't stop the German army from invading. Adolf Hitler, the leader of Nazi Germany, didn't think that Hungary was a reliable ally.

The Soviet Union eventually liberated Hungary, only to replace the Germans as the new foreign power in control of the country. For the next 45 years, until the early 1990s, the Soviets were in power. During this time Hungary was almost a closed country, very difficult to get in to or out of. Every aspect of daily life was closely watched by the Communist party, and those who disagreed with the system were imprisoned, executed, or they simply disappeared.

The cultural life and creativity of the Hungarian people was also tightly controlled. The passing on of traditional folk arts to children from their parents was discouraged. Instead, the government set up cultural groups to carefully control the artistic education of children. Today, at last, Hungary is a democratic nation that is just waking up to a new life of freedom and opportunities.

Despite invasion and occupation by other nations, Hungary has maintaned its rich culture. Music, literature, dance, cooking, embroidery, and pottery are a few of the traditions of the Hungarian people that have flourished, against all odds, through the ages.

Little lake Balaton below the town of Tihany

Lídia's mother and father, Ferencné and Ferenc

BARTH LÍDIA

Barth Lídia (in Hungary, the last name comes first) was born in 1941 in a part of Yugoslavia that before World War I was Hungarian territory.

I was a quiet child. I don't remember anymore the games I played then. I was happy with my baby doll. It was after World War II and children didn't play like they do now. It was very hard. From about the age of ten I did a lot of drawing. In drawing class at school, I did my work and also did some of my classmates' work for them!

Hers was not a typical childhood. Her mother was taken by the Nazis during the second world war and spent four years in a concentration camp. During that time Lídia and her father didn't know where she was.

At first when my mother came back I couldn't call her mama, because she had been gone so long and I was only two when she was taken. As I got older and began to understand what had happened, it made me very sad.

After the war, her father, who ran a small school, was briefly arrested by the Soviet communists. The school was closed and the family was thrown out of their home.

My father's school was a private secondary school. There were children of the wealthy and children of the poor, together. The tuition from the wealthy families helped pay for the education of the poorer ones. But when the communists came, the state took everything. We had to return to Hungary, because it was difficult for Hungarians living in Yugoslavia. My parents had to work very hard to build a new home.

Lídia's husband József and daughter Natália

32

Lídia's pottery shop

The family moved to Kaposvar, near Lake Balaton, where other family members lived.

During this time I didn't attend classes at a school. At that time it was dangerous for girls to travel, and the school was in another town. So my parents had me do my secondary school studies at home through correspondence.

Lídia's father became a bookkeeper at a factory that made ceramic furnaces.

At this point everything began for me. Because of what I saw at the company, I realized I wanted to be a ceramicist. I studied and learned about clay and ceramics at the company and ended up working there for several years.

At the age of 18, Lídia began showing her ceramic work. She quickly found recognition, winning prizes at various competitions.

Like drawing, ceramic work came naturally to me. At first I found it very interesting, and then I began to really love working with the clay.

When Lídia was 26, she married her husband, József, and they moved to Tihany (TEE-hahn) where they still live. In Tihany they bought two very old traditional houses that sit on a cliff overlooking Lake Balaton. They remodeled them into their home, ceramics studio, and shop.

They have two daughters, Lídia, 22, and Natália, 18. One is studying English at a university and the other is in secondary school. József also works with clay, having learned about ceramics from Lídia. He also manages their ceramics business. Lídia and he have been married and working together for 26 years.

He helps me with everything I do.

Lídia painting pottery

BRINGING LIFE TO CLAY

Lídia's passion for her artwork has been the guiding force in her life for more than thirty years. Along the way she experimented with various styles, but her path led her back to traditional Hungarian ceramics.

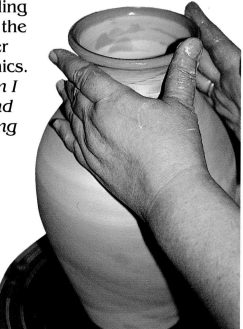

I began working with ceramics in 1957, when I was 16. I worked with a company until 1964 and then began working on my own. In the beginning I made modern ceramic pieces. But people weren't interested in them, so I changed to the traditional style, which I continue to do.

Lídia had to search to find the ceramic traditions of Hungary. This was not easy because Hungary sits between east and west and is a crossroads for many cultures.

Eventually I came upon the Haban (HAH-bahn) tradition. The Habans were a religious cult. Their ceramics date back to A.D. 1500. In those days only rich people had china.

Lídia spinning a clay pot

The development of the Haban culture helped bring ceramics to many people. I like the motifs and colors of Haban ceramics.

But Lídia didn't just copy the traditional styles, she added to it with her own ideas and techniques.

I wanted to see this simple, traditional ceramic form inside the modern houses. I also wanted to show another side of Haban ceramics. That's how

I arrived at the technique of using white background with blue paint and blue background with white paint.

In developing and refining her style she decided to visit other countries and learn from their traditions and innovations.

I visited ceramics companies in

Lídia and József working in their studio

József putting plates in the oven

Czechoslovakia, Poland, East Germany, and Denmark. I brought back experience and new techniques. But the motifs I still make with a traditional stick.

The process of making ceramics has many steps and takes a lot of time. Each step must be carried out with great care and attention to detail.

I start with the wet clay. I spin it on the potting wheel and shape it with my hands into a pot or plate or whatever I am making. Then it must dry a little. Then I spin it again, and with special knives I trim the edges and smooth out rough spots. It then dries, very slowly, and after that it goes into the oven for the first time.

After it comes out of the oven and cools, it is painted. Then it goes into the oven again, at 1,000° centigrade. When it comes out and cools, it's finished. When we open the oven we don't know what it will look like. We have an idea, but we don't know for sure. It's nice to open the oven and see how beautiful the pieces are.

For Lídia each day is an adventure in creating something new and re-creating something very old.

When I am working I am able to relax and switch off other things around me and in my mind. I never felt that I must do this work, or that I need to do it. I love to do it. I think that there are only a few people in the world who can do something they really love. I love what I do and what I make. I feel very lucky.

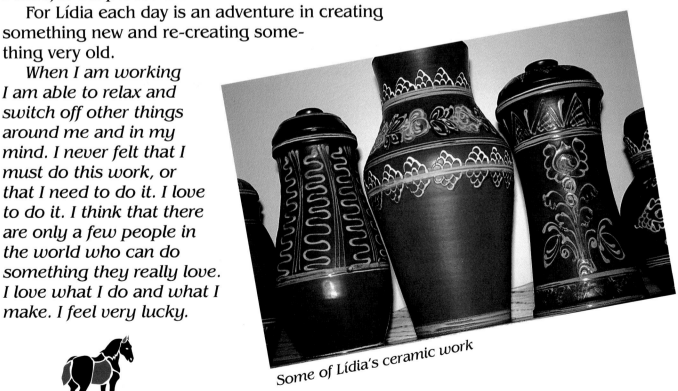

Some of Lídia's ceramic work

LOVE WHAT YOU DO

Lídia had more difficulties in the first ten years of her life than most people face in a whole lifetime. Despite these problems she was able to make a creative life filled with beauty. No one can really tell you what you should do with your life, or how you should solve your own problems. But Lídia's ideas might help you find some answers for yourself.

Love what you do, no matter what it is, whether it is art or something else. You must love what you do. Call on your teachers and your parents to help you find what you're looking for.

Art and family are the two most important parts of Lídia's life. One would not mean much without the other.

Take time alone to make things, but balance your alone time by spending time with your family. I think it's a problem with this generation that the parents don't have enough time to care for their children. And the children don't have time to learn how to create things.

Between schoolwork, television, sleeping, and eating, there seems to be hardly enough time in the day to try new creative things. But the secret all artists share is that making art can be better than TV, sleeping, and sometimes even eating! Creating can give you a feeling of freedom. If you try it, you just might find the same beauty that Lídia has.

It is beautiful to create. Bring love to your making of art.

ACTIVITY PAGE

CLAY CREATION

Here is something you can do that is similar to what Lídia does. You can make things from clay.

You will need the following things:
- One or two cans of Play-Doh.™
- A plastic or dull metal knife.
- Colored markers, crayons, or paints and a brush.
- A cookie sheet for baking.

Step 1. Decide what you'd like to make with the clay, perhaps a small plate or bowl, a heart, or some letters that spell your name, "Mom," or something else.

Step 2. Put your clay on a smooth, clean surface, such as a counter top. Begin to mold the clay into what you want to make. If you're making a plate, flatten the clay out first, but don't make it too thin. If you want to make letters, flatten the clay first, trace the outline of the letters, then cut them out with your knife. Once you've molded the clay into the shape you want, trim off any extra clay with the knife and smooth out the rough spots along the edges.

Step 3. Ask an adult to help you with this step. Set the temperature on the oven to 200 degrees. Put your clay creation on a cookie sheet and bake it in the oven for about 20 minutes. If you start to see cracks while it's baking, take it out early. Don't leave the room while the oven is on. When taking the tray out, use a pot holder to keep from burning yourself.

Step 4. Let your clay creation cool for 30 minutes. Then decorate it whatever way you like with your colors or paint. Make it colorful or dark or bright. If you enjoyed this activity, try it again.

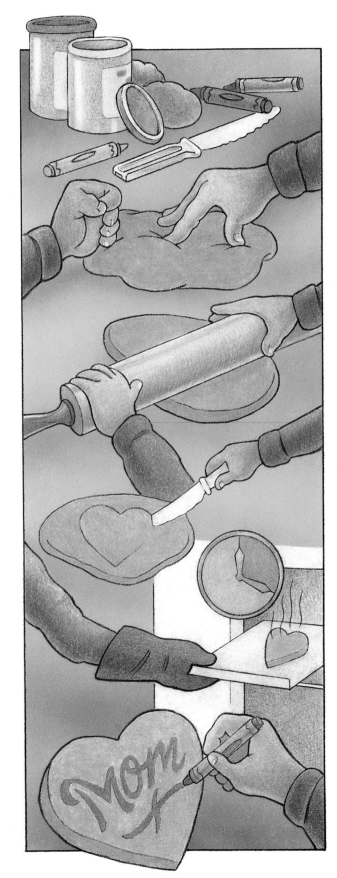

LARS PIRAK
of Sápmi

THE SAAMI LAND AND PEOPLE

In the far northern reaches of Europe, above and below the Arctic Circle, is the land of Sápmi (SOP-mee). Here live the Saami (SAW-mee) people. Also known as Lapps, they are a tribe whose roots go back to the first humans who settled here 10,000 years ago. In this land of the summer midnight sun and the winter midday stars, they carry on a way of life that is closer to the traditional Native American way of life than it is to modern Europeans'.

Theirs is a land of great lakes, sparkling streams, and endless pine forests. The Saamis gather from nature the gifts that allow them to survive. Their living mythology speaks of father Sun, mother Earth, and the god of wind. The traditional Saami religion honors all things as living beings. Deep respect for nature has always been part of the Saami way.

For many thousands of years these people had almost no contact with the rest of Europe. Great distances and harsh winters added to the Saamis'

"When I work I feel connected to all the universe. In some special places I get a feeling for the ancestors. I gather my materials in the same places that my ancestors found them."

—Lars Pirak

Saami reindeer

38

cultural isolation. Christianity didn't come to the Saamis until the 1600s. As a result, they form an important link with the past that cannot be found anywhere else in Europe.

A family walking on an ice-covered lake

Over the past century, the Saamis have begun to adopt more modern lifestyles. But their traditional ways are still strong. Modern Saami schools and cultural centers teach and preserve the language, the history, and the handicrafts of the tribe. More importantly, Saami mothers and fathers still pass on to their children the old ways of living.

The basis of the Saami way has always been hunting and fishing. The reindeer is the most important animal to them. From the reindeer the Saamis get meat, fur for clothing and boots, skin for drum heads, and antlers for carving into tools. Some of the reindeer are used for pulling sleds, and the female reindeer gives milk. Until a few hundred years ago the reindeer were hunted like the bear, fox, and other wild animals. But the Saamis learned to tame and herd the reindeer.

Today, Sápmi is not recognized as a nation in itself. The kings and political leaders of Norway, Sweden, Finland, and Russia believe the land of Sápmi belongs to their countries. Over many centuries they have used economic and military force to control and colonize Sápmi. As a result, the Saami people do not rule themselves.

The Saamis have fought nonviolently for their rights. Recently, they have made much progress. But the process is slow, and in the meantime the use of their lands continues without their approval. The Saamis believe this land is rightfully theirs. They have taken care of it, and it has taken care of them since before any of the modern European nations existed.

A winter forest

Lars and his wife Astrid

LARS PIRAK

Lars Pirak (PEA-rahk) was born in 1932 and grew up in the tiny village of Loqvalqokta (loh-VAH-lohk-tah), which means "little house where you keep things." The village was on a small bay, deep in the arctic wilderness.

The family's log home, built by Lars' grandfather, was the only house in the village. There was no electricity or indoor plumbing. Only about six or seven people lived in the village during the coldest part of winter. A group of families, who followed the reindeer herds, came

through at the same time each year and lived there in Saami teepees and huts. During the annual reindeer round-up, as many as a hundred people would stay in the village.

Lars' childhood was spent playing and learning in nature. In the forest around his village there were moose, bear, fox, wolf, lynx, eagle, hawk, and falcon. And, of course, there were reindeer.

As a child I skied a lot. Often I would have a reindeer pull me on the skis. Sometimes we played reindeer herding games and tried to rope the reindeer. The other children and I had a small herd of reindeer that we played herding games with. We played and learned at the same time. In the summer we fished and swam in the bay.

In the Saami culture there is the very old religious tradition of the *nojd* (noid). The nojd is the shaman, or medicine man, of the tribe. For a long time the nojds were outlawed and killed, often burned, by the Christian government of Sweden. So the nojds did their work in great secrecy.

Lars' son Mikael and his grandson

There was an old man who lived in my village who was a good storyteller. He could look at your hand and tell you how your life would go. He didn't wear shoes, even when it was very cold outside. This man taught me about the Saami medicine men, or nojds. When I was 12 he took me to a big cave in the mountains called the "sacrifice door." The medicine men went there to call the spirits. They sacrificed reindeer to the gods and painted the rocks with the reindeer blood.

Students making traditional handicrafts at a Saami school

An icy stream

The old man fell down on his knees in this cave. He turned his head and said something into a hole in the rock on his left side. A few hours passed and I heard his voice come out of a hole on the right side. Then the old man passed out.

Lars left his village in 1955 when he married his wife, Astrid. He was 23 years old. They have two daughters and a son. He now lives in the town of Jokkmokk (YAHK-mahk). Today no one lives in the village where Lars grew up, but the old log house is still there.

Throughout his life Lars has done many different kinds of work. Among other things he was a reindeer herder, a lumberjack, and a vegetable picker. But during all these times he was first of all a maker, an artist.

THE MAGIC MAKER

Over the years Lars has worked with many different artistic materials, called mediums. He paints with oils and watercolors, draws with ink and pencil, and carves reindeer horn and wood. He sculpts wood, clay, steel, and bronze. He creates with ceramics, does metalsmithing, and makes furniture inlaid with wood. He has also written plays, songs, poetry, and done acting. But his first love has always been the traditional handicraft of his people and his family.

Many of the pieces that Lars makes now, from reindeer horn and wood, were not always considered art. When he was young they were used as a part of daily life for storing food or as tools. Lars learned the traditional Saami handicrafts from his family and from the old people in the village.

The old man who took me to the cave also carved things. He carved reindeers and dogs and small Saami teepees. This man was an inspiration to me. I never thought to keep his work, but maybe it is still there in the old house.

Lars carving in his workshop

As a child Lars loved to draw.

I started drawing in the first grade and found it very interesting. We didn't have paper, so I used bark from the birch tree and I drew with coal. When I was about 12 I did my first wood sculptures with knives. I didn't start painting until I was 15. I sent away for a correspondence course in art. The mailman got very angry, because it was a huge package and he had to bring it to me on skis!

In his teens Lars was already selling his wood sculptures, knives, and jewelry.

I feel great happiness when I make the things of my people. It is a pleasure to know that my mother and

Lars carving a reindeer milk bowl

![Lars carving a reindeer milk bowl]

Lars carving a reindeer milk bowl

sister will use the bowl to take the milk from the reindeer. But it should have beauty too. So I inlay the reindeer horn into the bowl and make it more beautiful.

When I work I feel connected to all the universe. Sometimes my thoughts travel off. In some special places I get a feeling for the ancestors. I gather my materials in the same places that my ancestors found them. When I am out in the mountains painting, I think of my people who have been crossing this country for so long. I wonder what they were thinking about.

Lars is now over 60 years old. He has accomplished much in his life. His work has been shown in many countries. He is a highly respected artist in the Saami tradition. Yet he has another creative passion that he hopes to pursue in the coming years.

One of my biggest dreams right now is to write a novel. I want to write about the nojds and about the time when I was growing up. When I was young it used to take as long as 15 days to travel from Jokkmokk to my home in the mountains. Today it only takes an hour by car. By helicopter it takes seven minutes! I want to write about the old times, the new times, and growing up in the middle of it all.

Lars' handicrafts are made from wood, reindeer antler, and metal

43

HONOR NATURE

Lars has been very fortunate. He grew up in nature and learned the old ways of his people. He uses his knowledge to guide him through the modern world. Listening to him speak about his life is like hearing a voice from the past.

The Saami people live close to nature. I want you to honor nature. Modern people should think about the future. That will help you have a better life and make you more stable.

Creating is one of the ways you can honor nature and prepare for the future.

Use your thoughts and think about the handicrafts. Learn how to be calm and let the things you make grow in your hands. It can give you great joy in your life to make things from nature. If you look at things made from nature, you will see they are living materials. The beauty should have its own part too.

You and your family also have ancient traditions. You may not know them now, but they are there if you want to find them.

It is very important that you know about the traditions of your people. These traditions can make an easier life for you. The Native Americans still have a living culture, they still have their traditions. It is important to have parents that care about traditions and try to show them. They should also teach the traditions in the schools and talk about the old times. If you don't know your traditions, you can look in old books and museums. You can go out into nature and look to nature for answers.

Lars with the first bowl he ever carved

CARVING ART FROM NATURE

When Lars was young he did simple carvings. You can carve, too. *Ask an adult to help you with this activity.*

You will need the following things:
- A small wood saw.
- A knife.
- Colored markers, crayons, or paints and a brush.

Step 1. Find a tree with green leaves that has some small branches you can reach. Choose a branch that looks special to you. The branch should be no more than two inches wide and two feet long. Cut the branch off at its base. If it's not your tree, get permission first.

Step 2. Hold the branch under water for about 5 minutes until it's soft and easy to cut.

Step 3. Starting at one end peel the bark from the branch. Go slowly and peel away from your body, being careful not to bring the knife too close to yourself. The bark should come off easily. As you peel you will begin to see the smooth surface under the bark. Peel all the bark off so the stick is smooth.

Step 4. Now use the knife to cut pieces out of the branch or notch designs on it. Or you can leave it bare and smooth. Sometimes a simple branch without any bark is a piece of art.

Step 5. Choose colors you think would look good on the stick. You can draw things on the stick or just color it. Sometimes a little color is enough, or you can use lots of colors. You can also tie ribbons, twine, or special things to it. When you finish, show it to your family and friends. Maybe you'd like to give it to someone you love.

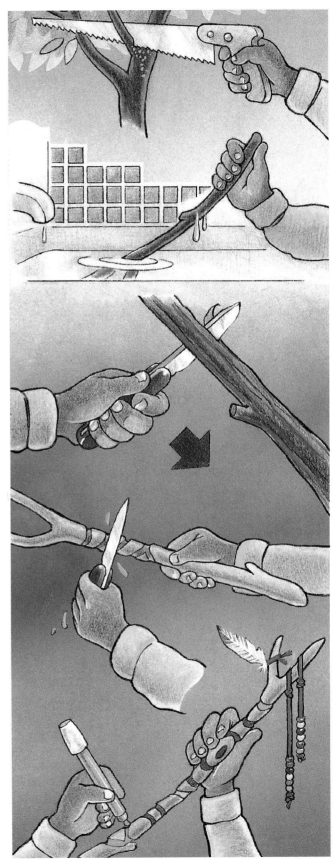

45

Arctic—the region around the North Pole, 40

Abstract art—art that does not represent things with pictures but expresses the artist's ideas or feelings, 15

Ancestors—any of the persons from whom a person is descended, 9, 15, 43

Arrangement—to adapt a musical composition for voices and instruments, 27

Banshee—a female spirit whose wail is said to foretell a death in a house, 7

Celts—an ancient tribe of European people, 7, 23

Civilization—a developed, organized society, 15

Concentration camp—a place where political prisoners are imprisoned, 32

Confederacy—a union of people or states, 23

Culture—the traditions, art, social structure, values, and beliefs of a group of people, 5, 7, 23, 31

Folklore—the traditional beliefs, tales, etc. of a community, 7

Gaelic—ancient language of Irish and Scottish Celts, 7

Germanic—having German charecteristics, 23

Glacier—a river of ice that moves very slowly, 24

Handicraft—work that requires both skill with the hands and artistic design, 15, 39, 42, 44

Homogenized—something whose parts are all the same, not diverse, 9

Innovator—a person who introduces a new way of doing things, 15

Leprechaun—an elf who looks like a very small old man, 7

Liberate—to set free, especially from an oppressive authority, 31

Lumberjack—a person whose trade is cutting timber, 41

Medium—the material or form used by an artist, 18, 42

Migrate—to leave one place and settle in another, 7

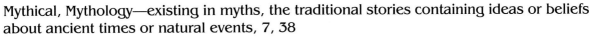

Mythical, Mythology—existing in myths, the traditional stories containing ideas or beliefs about ancient times or natural events, 7, 38

Native American—the original inhabitants of North America, 5, 38, 44

Nomads—tribes of people who move from place to place, 6

Profession—an occupation, 10

Rainbow Warriors—people of all different races who share a love for the Earth, a desire for a better world, and a willingness to work for both, 4, 5

Romansch—Alpine dialects that come from the ancient language of Latin, spoken in East Switzerland, 23

Shaman—a priest claiming to have contact with the gods, 40

Traditions, Traditional—information, beliefs, and customs passed from one generation to another, 5, 9, 10, 15, 18, 27, 28, 34, 35, 38, 39, 40, 42, 43, 44

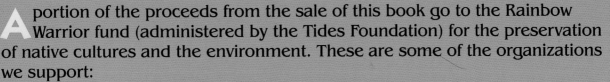

A portion of the proceeds from the sale of this book go to the Rainbow Warrior fund (administered by the Tides Foundation) for the preservation of native cultures and the environment. These are some of the organizations we support:

    The Huichol Cultural Center, Santiago, Mexico
    Lighthawk: The Environmental Air Force, Santa Fe, New Mexico
    Native Lifeways: Oneida Nation, Amherst, New York

COMMUNICATE

Let us know what you think. Write to the artists. Send poetry, pictures, stories, whatever. Send your name and address. We will put you on our mailing list. Write, right now!

Rainbow Warrior
P.O. Box 9858
Santa Fe, New Mexico 87504

BIZARRE & BEAUTIFUL SERIES

A spirited and fun investigation of the mysteries of the five senses in the animal kingdom.

Each title in the series is 8½" x 11", $14.95 hardcover, with color photographs and illustrations throughout.

Bizarre & Beautiful Ears
Bizarre & Beautiful Eyes
Bizarre & Beautiful Feelers
Bizarre & Beautiful Noses
Bizarre & Beautiful Tongues

RAINBOW WARRIOR SERIES

W hat is a Rainbow Warrior Artist? It is a person who strives to live in harmony with the Earth and all living creatures, and who tries to better the world while living his or her life in a creative way.

Each title is written by Reavis Moore with a foreword by LeVar Burton, and is 8½" x 11", 48 pages, $14.95 hardcover, with color photographs and illustrations.

Native Artists of Africa
Native Artists of North America
Native Artists of Europe (available 9/94)

 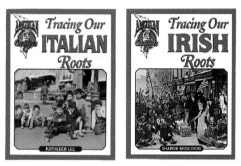

ROUGH AND READY SERIES

L earn about the men and women who settled the American West. Explore the myths and legends about these courageous individuals and learn about the environmental, cultural, and economic legacies they left to us.

Each title in the series is written by A. S. Gintzler and is 48 pages, 8½" x 11", $12.95 hardcover, with two-color illustrations and duotone archival photographs.

	Available 7/94:
Rough and Ready Cowboys	**Rough and Ready Loggers**
Rough and Ready Homesteaders	**Rough and Ready**
Rough and Ready Prospectors	**Outlaws & Lawmen**
	Rough and Ready Railroaders

AMERICAN ORIGINS SERIES

M any of us are the third and fourth generation of our families to live in America. Learn what our great-great-grandparents experienced when they arrived here and how much of our lives are still intertwined with theirs.

Each title is 48 pages, 8½" x 11", $12.95 hardcover, with two-color illustrations and duotone archival photographs.

	Available 6/94:
Tracing Our German Roots	**Tracing Our Chinese Roots**
Tracing Our Irish Roots	**Tracing Our Japanese Roots**
Tracing Our Italian Roots	**Tracing Our Polish Roots**
Tracing Our Jewish Roots	